# Me and My Pet

# Dogs

How to train your owner!

## Heather Maisner

OXFORD

# OXFORD
## UNIVERSITY PRESS

Great Clarendon Street, Oxford OX2 6DP

Oxford University Press is a department of the University of Oxford.
It furthers the University's objective of excellence in research, scholarship,
and education by publishing worldwide in

Oxford   New York

Auckland   Cape Town   Dar es Salaam   Hong Kong   Karachi
Kuala Lumpur   Madrid   Melbourne   Mexico City   Nairobi
New Delhi   Shanghai   Taipei   Toronto

With offices in

Argentina   Austria   Brazil   Chile   Czech Republic   France   Greece
Guatemala   Hungary   Italy   Japan   Poland   Portugal   Singapore
South Korea   Switzerland   Thailand   Turkey   Ukraine   Vietnam

Oxford is a registered trade mark of Oxford University Press
in the UK and in certain other countries

British Library Cataloguing in Publication Data

Data available

ISBN-13: 978-0-19-911581-5

1 3 5 7 9 10 8 6 4 2

Printed in Singapore by Imago

# MEET JESSIE

Name:     Jessie Martin
Age:      4 months
Breed:    Golden Retriever
Lives:    Brighton, England
Owners:   Fred and Emily Martin,
          ages 5 and 10

I am writing this for Fred and Emily and their friends,
so that they understand me and we can all live happily together.

*Jessie*

# Look at me!

I'm Jessie the Golden Retriever and I love being part of a family. I live in a big house with a garden, with Fred and Emily. I make a very good pet. I like playing and having fun, and running across the fields.

I have strong **jaws** and my **teeth** are sharp and pointed for eating meat.

I have a long **nose** and a keen sense of smell. I use my nose to check my surroundings and send scent messages to my friends.

Dogs' noses are all different shapes

My hunter's **eyes** are good at spotting movement and seeing in dim light.

I prick up my **ears** to help me hear. I lift up my ears when I am happy.

My long **nose** gives me a good sense of smell.

I have a deep **chest** with a strong heart and lungs.

My strong **muscles** let me move in all directions.

I wag my **tail** when I am happy and when I'm talking to my friends. It also helps me to balance as I run.

My **body** is built to run over long distances. I trot along at a steady pace but sometimes I speed up and run very, very fast in short bursts.

I have two layers of **fur** – a soft undercoat and a tough top coat.

Dogs' ears come in many different shapes and sizes.

# Different Breeds

There are more than 100 different kinds of dog, called breeds. We vary in size and shape more than any other animals. We can be big or small, with long or short coats, and upright or floppy ears. We can move very fast or be lazy and slow. Over the centuries, people have bred dogs for different jobs: we can guard, herd and hunt, and we help the blind and disabled. Whatever we look like, we will always be your friend. If you want a dog as a pet, be careful to choose the right dog for you.

I'm a **Golden Retriever**, bred to be a gun dog, working with hunters and sniffing out game. I'm playful and fun but I need space and exercise.

Timmy the **Border Collie** is a herding dog. His long hair keeps him warm outside. He has a 'strong eye' and they say he can control sheep just by glaring at them. He's light, fast and obedient.

Winnie the **West Highland Terrier** is a hunting dog. She was bred to follow prey underground. The word terrier comes from Latin 'terra', which means earth. She's small and lively and a fantastic watch dog, always alert. She's intelligent, easy to train and good with strangers.

Dilly the **Deerhound** loves to go over hill and dale for miles. She will love you forever but if you leave her alone, she'll be very sad and lonely.

Lucy the **King Charles Spaniel** is a lapdog, a miniature, easy to carry around. She's lively and intelligent and can live in a flat or small house but needs lots of cuddles. She likes to be the centre of attention.

Gilly the **Greyhound** can follow a scent for miles and miles. She never wants to come home and needs lots of outdoor space.

Karen the **Husky** is very strong, with a deep coat to keep out the cold. She pulls sledges in the snow and can go places where no other transport is able to go.

Alf the **mongrel** is a mixture of several breeds. He's warm and friendly and loves being in a family. He's good natured, easy and intelligent.

# My family

Dogs have lots of relatives living out in the wild all over the world. They belong to a group of animals called canines.

### My cousin the Wolf
Wolves look after their babies and go hunting together in a group called a pack. They are family animals, living in the wilderness, the hills and the forest.

### My cousin the Arctic Fox
He lives in the Arctic, where the ground is frozen and it is very, very cold. He has a thick coat which even covers the soles of his feet to protect him from harsh ice and snow.

### My cousin the Maned Wolf
He has very long legs. He lives in South America and likes to hunt small animals including rodents, snails and slugs.

**My cousin the Jackal**
She lives in Africa and Asia and eats whatever she can find, from fruit and vegetables to creepy crawlies.

**My cousin the Red Fox**
Foxes are adventurous and fearless. They come into the city looking for food and sometimes make a den in a park or back garden.

Dogs living in the wild adapt to all sorts of environments. Unlike pet dogs, they know how to take care of themselves. Most wild dogs hunt in packs and share the kill. There is always a dominant male in the pack.

**My cousin the Raccoon Dog**
He comes from east Asia. He slows down when the weather is cold. In China, he is hunted for his warm coat.

**My cousin the Dingo**
The only wild dog of Australia, he hunts at night and cannot bark.

# I am born

A female dog is called a bitch. When my mum became pregnant, her body changed. Her stomach grew big and round. Her owner prepared a big basket with paper and blankets and put it in a warm, quiet place. When my mum was ready to have her babies, she lay down in the basket.

I was born with a brother and a sister. Our mum licked each one of us as we were born. I crawled up close to her and suckled her milk. I could smell but I couldn't see or hear. I just wanted to sleep and eat.

At about four weeks, we learned to **play**. We **jumped** all over each other and **squealed** and **yelped**. Sometimes we slept in a bundle and our mum went for a walk to stretch her legs and eat.

Newborn puppies depend fully on their mother. Their eyes and ears are **sealed shut**. Eyes and ears begin to open after 2 weeks but do not function properly until about 4 weeks. If the mother is calm and happy, the puppies will be, too. If she is nervous, she could make her puppies nervous, too.

Puppies should stay with their mother for at least 8 weeks.
Puppies who leave too early can be nervous and difficult to train.

Our mum **taught** us lots of things:
She taught us where to go to the toilet.
She taught us not to stray too far.
She taught us that people are our friends.

We stayed with our mum for about 10 weeks.

The number of pups in a litter varies. Small breeds, like **Chihuahuas** and **Dachshunds** (below), usually have two or three pups. A **Mastiff** could have up to twenty pups – too many for the mother to feed, so some have to be fed with a bottle.

**Dalmations** are born without any spots. The spots begin to appear at about 2 weeks. **Yorkshire Terriers** are black when they are born.

# Choosing our owners

If you are my owner, I will be your best friend. I will listen to your stories, when you are happy or sad, and I will never criticise you. Please listen to me, too. I am friendly, obedient and faithful.

Puppies and dogs are all quite different. When you pick one to be your pet, you need to understand its personality and needs.

A **puppy** is easy to train into your household.

An **adult** is already **trained** and **obedient**. If you take an adult for a walk, he should behave well.

If you want a pure-bred puppy (pedigree) to take to shows, you should go to a specialist breeder. If you want an older dog, who is already trained, it is best to go to an animal shelter.

TIPS ON CHOOSING A PET
Choose a healthy puppy with a good coat, clear eyes and wet nose. Choose a puppy who is happy running about. *Do not* choose a puppy who looks ill and unhealthy, or one who seems very restless and nervous.

Fred and Emily brought me home in a **pet carrier**. Fred talked to me in a quiet voice all the way home, so I didn't feel nervous.
Emily opened the box and left me to look around before lifting me out into my new home.
It was **strange** coming into a new house. I was **alone** for the first time ever. I was in a new place, without my mum and my brothers and sisters. At first, Fred and Emily stayed with me most of the time. At night, they left the radio or TV on, so that I could hear voices and didn't feel lonely.

To hold your puppy, put one hand under her bottom and the other around her chest. Never squeeze her. Just hold her close and speak gently.

# I'm a fast learner

When I came to live with Fred and Emily, I didn't know my name. They called me lots of times when they played with me – 'Jessie, come here'. They knelt on the floor with their arms out, as they called me, so I didn't jump up. They called me, when it was time to eat – 'Jessie, dinner time!' And when it was time to go to bed – 'Bedtime, Jessie.' I quickly learned my name.

Emily **spoke firmly** when she wanted me to sit. '**Sit!**' She fussed over me when I got it right.

Fred spoke firmly when he wanted me to walk close behind him. '**Heel!**' He stroked and patted me when I got it right.

My owners never ever shout at me, even when I'm naughty. And they never hit me. Fred frowns and Emily speaks sternly – '**Stop**' - and I immediately understand.

When we dogs meet, we **sniff** and **lick** one another to say hello.

To toilet train me, Emily and Fred took me outside many times a day — when I woke up in the morning, each time after I'd eaten and always before I went to bed.

Sometimes there was an accident. I was so busy playing, I didn't think of going outside until it was too late. Fred frowned but he was never cross. When I did the right thing, Emily and Fred smiled and said, "**Well done!**"

Throw a ball and get your dog to bring it back. This helps it to be obedient and understand that you are the boss.

The way dogs respond to people is linked to the way they used to behave in the wild. A dog sees its family as a pack, with you or one of your parents as the leader. If it isn't trained well, it may try to become leader.

# I like my food

I love eating, like all dogs. I dream about food when I'm asleep and I look forward to food after my walk. I like to eat four small meals a day.

A puppy can have four small meals a day An adult dog needs only one big meal a day. Do not give your puppy too many treats or he will get fat.

I love to **chew** on a real meat **bone** with marrow inside. I also like bone-shaped chews. They keep my teeth strong and clean. Never give me little cooked bones because these could make me choke.

I like titbits as a reward when I am good. I can eat your meat **leftovers** without bones.

I **pant** when I am hot and thirsty.

**Never** take my food away from me when I am eating. This will make me angry and I'll **growl** at you.

I have a **special bowl** for my **food** and another special bowl for **water**. They are always kept in the same place.

Feed your puppy at the same time each day. Keep the food bowl in one place. Wash the food bowl after she has eaten. Fill the water bowl with fresh water and keep it topped up.

Puppies drink milk from their mother for 4 to 5 weeks. Then they eat puppy food. When they are fully grown, they need to eat adult food.

17

# When I'm happy

We use our bodies, especially our tails, to show our emotions. I wag my tail when I am pleased to see you and when I meet up with friends.

When I want to play, I crouch down and push my back and tail high into the air. This is called a play-bow. I open my mouth and relax my face. This is how I invite you and my friends to play.

When I meet new friends, I sniff them first. This is my way of greeting them.

Sometimes we **roll on to our backs** because we want you to play. We are in a happy mood and will not hurt you. It means we know you are the boss. It may also mean we want you to **stroke our tummies**.

When my owners are not at home, they leave lots of things for me to **play** with. They also leave me things to chew. I especially need things to **chew** when my teeth are growing.

We're happy when we have a **ball** to play with.

We're happy when we play **tug of war**.

Sometimes when I'm happy, I may **bite** you by mistake. Please don't be angry. Just say 'N o' in a firm voice.

When I lived with my brothers and sisters, we sometimes **pretended** to **fight**. But we were just playing happily. We would never hurt one another.

# Keep away!

I have lots of different moods and feelings, just like you. I use my body to let people and other dogs know what I am feeling.

When I'm frightened, I flatten my ears against my head and drop my tail between my legs. Keep away! I may bite you to protect myself.

When I am eating, keep away! If you come too close or suddenly come up from behind me, I may think you are going to take my bowl away and snap at you.

When I am **very angry**, I hold my tail straight and the fur on my neck stands up.

If I'm asleep and you approach me suddenly, I may **snap** at you.

Remember, although your puppy loves you very much, sometimes she needs **time on her own**.

I cannot talk but I have many ways of showing how I feel. I can **bark**, **growl**, **howl**, **whine** and **yelp**. I bark to warn off enemies.

I growl to ask you to play and also when I feel aggressive.

If a dog howls, it means it is sad and lonely and wants someone to come and find it.

If I bark loudly at you, I'm telling you to keep away.

If I **curl back my lips** and **show my teeth**, keep away! This means I may bite.

If I don't want to let go of something, I may growl. **Be careful!**

I **howl** to other dogs and family far away, when I cannot see them and feel **lonely**.

An **untrained** dog, who is frightened, will attack to defend itself. A **nervous** dog can snap, nip and bite.

If a dog is going to attack, it shows clear signals beforehand. It stands very tall with ears and tail held high. It bares its teeth and stares in a threatening way. Keep away!

# When I'm tired

I need a comfy bed in a quiet place without draughts. Although I may get dirty and muddy, I like my bed to be kept clean. Sometimes, my bed will need treating for fleas.

Puppies like to sleep in a cosy box or basket lined with bedding. Always keep the bed in the same place, so your puppy knows where to go. Let him feel that this is his own special territory. You can treat the bedding for fleas with a special spray from the vet.

I need my **bed** to be in a corner **away from draughts**. Draughts can give me colds and flu.

I like a nice, cosy **blanket** or an old sweater for my bedding.

We love **chewing** everything around us. Make sure the bedding is made of material we can't easily chew.

Tiny puppies love to sleep curled up together in a bundle.

Keep electrical wires out of the way – puppies love to chew these, too. And they'll chew anything you leave about, so be sure to put your favourite toys away.

My friend Bertie is getting old now, so he wears a little **coat** for extra warmth.

If I'm asleep, don't make a loud noise near me. I'll be frightened when I wake up and I'll growl and snap at you. If I'm tired for a long time, it could be that I'm not feeling very well. You need to take me to the vet.

# Training and exercise

I have lots of energy and need to go for walks in the park or across the fields every day. If I don't exercise, I'll get fat, lazy and bored. I like being with people and other puppies, and I enjoy being trained. If you praise me, I can do lots of things. I've learned to wear a collar and a tag with my name, address and telephone number on it. I've learned to walk on a lead.

At puppy school, I'm learning to play with other puppies. We learn together, using our voices, faces and bodies.

Teach your puppy the most important commands: to come when called, to sit, lie down, stay and walk to heel. Keep titbits in your pocket as rewards. You can buy dried food treats at the pet shop.

Some of my friends are so well trained, they can do amazing things:

Floppy the **Cocker Spaniel** was bred as a gun dog. He's happy and intelligent and helps the police search for drugs and weapons.

Sam the **St Bernard** rescues people from mountains and lakes.

Rex the **Retriever** is calm and helpful. He acts as eyes for a blind man.

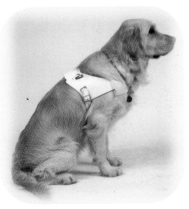

Molly the **German Shepherd** helps track criminals.

# Washing and grooming

I love to play in the dirt and mud but I'm not very good at keeping myself clean, so I need your help. My coat is short. I need grooming at least once a week. My friend Barker the long-haired Dachshund, needs grooming every day, or his hair becomes matted, and then it hurts when you brush him.

You need a special brush and comb for your dog. Ask at the pet shop which type is best. Always brush gently in the direction of the fur. Start with the back, then brush the legs, the tummy and the head.

I try to sit still when I am **brushed**, but sometimes it tickles. I love to roll on my back so that my tummy can be brushed too. My friend Sid the Red Setter likes to stand while he is brushed.

A dog **comb** is good for getting out tangles.
A special bristle **brush** is good for long or short hair.
A **corder** is good for brushing out dead fur.

I need a **bath** regularly. Fred and Emily bathe me together. First, they brush me. Emily holds me still while Fred scoops water over my back. They use special **dog shampoo** and rub it in. It tickles but I like it. Then they rinse it all off. I stand up and **shake** the water out of my fur. They lift me out of the bath and wipe me down with an **old towel**.

After a bath, always keep your dog inside so that he doesn't catch a cold.

# Keeping healthy

I have bright eyes, a wet nose and a healthy coat.
I love being stroked, hugged and brushed.

Your puppy needs a full check-up
when he is 12 weeks
old, before he goes
out walking in
the street.

When my friend
Dotty the Dalmatian
went to the vet for the first time,
he looked at her eyes, ears,
teeth and fur to make sure
she was healthy. He gave
her some injections
against disease.

A dog needs to have injections once a
year to keep it protected against disease.

The first time I went to the **vet**, I went there in the pet carrier. Now, I go on the lead. If I sit very quietly and don't eat or if I keep trying to stretch, it may be that my **tummy** is upset. Give me lots of fresh water to drink and take me to the vet.

If I start to **limp**, I may have a thorn or a splinter in my foot or I may have broken my leg. I will need to see the vet.

If my eyes are **sore** and **runny**, I may have a cold and will need to see the vet.

When your puppy is six months old, it can have a small operation to stop it from having puppies or from fathering puppies. Remember, if you WANT your pet to have puppies, you'll need lots of good homes for them.

If I start **scratching** a lot, I may have **fleas**.
Fleas are very annoying and make me irritable.
The vet has sprays and medicine to get rid of them.

If your puppy starts eating a lot but losing weight, he may have worms. He needs to go to the vet for some pills.

# Goodbye!

I've loved writing this book;
I hope it's helped you understand
what makes me happy!

Jessie

# FIND OUT MORE

Some useful websites:

www.pdsa.org.uk

www.bbc.co.uk/cbbc/wild/pets

www.dogstrust.org.uk

All images © DK.